So, You Want to Be a Doctor- When You Grow Up?

A Children's Career Book Series.

Author: Lam Do, M.D.

Illustrator: Cuc Anh

You can grow up and be anything you want to be!

So, you want to be a doctor?

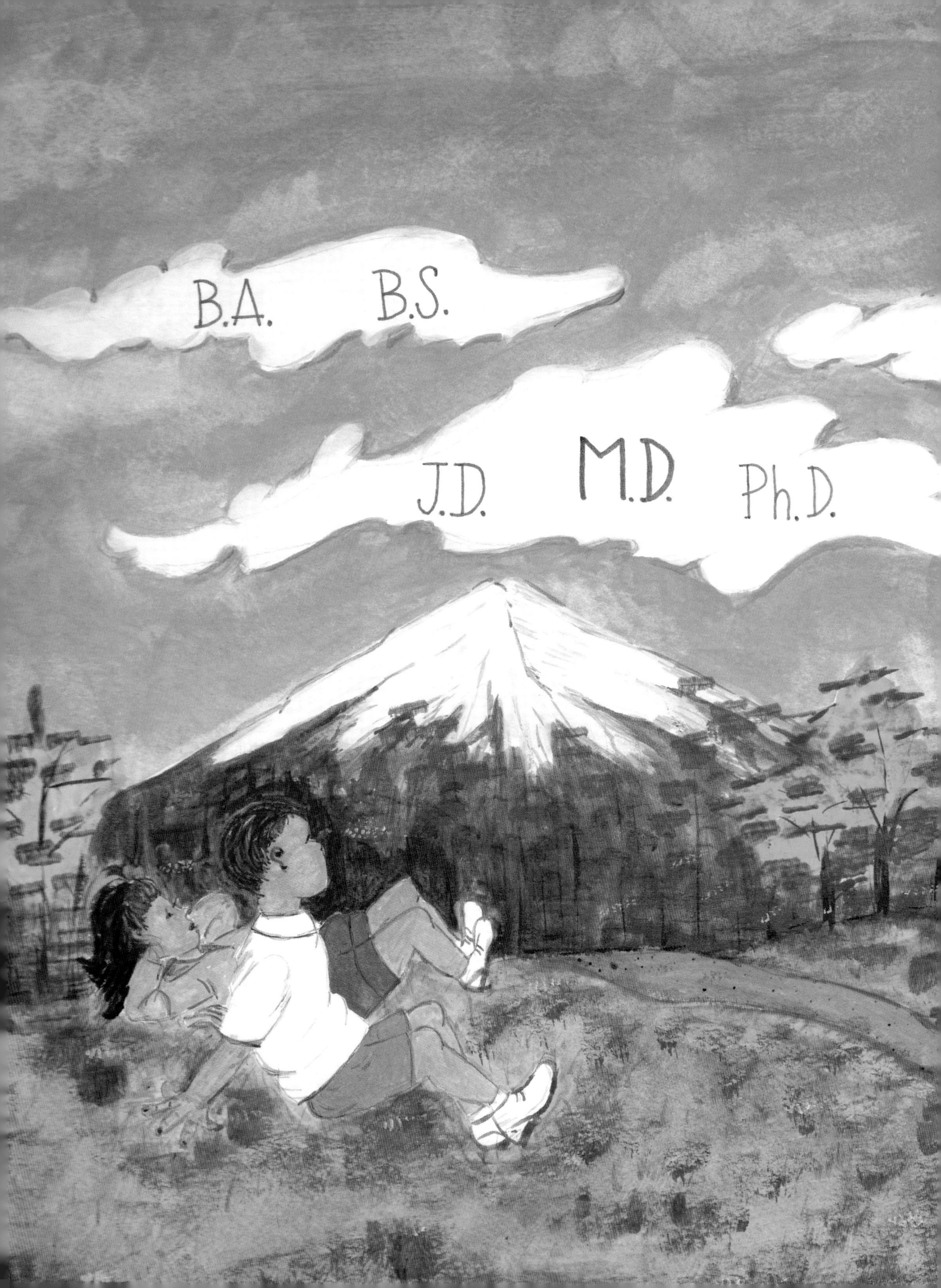
B.A. B.S.
J.D. M.D. Ph.D.

You must love helping people with all your heart.

This is how... You put your dreams up in the clouds.

Each and everyday, you build your ladder.

Up, up and away... Higher and higher you'll go.

Believe it or not, you'll be in the clouds someday.

This is the recipe... For what you want to be.

Recipe for Making a DOCTOR!

Ingredients:

1 child who loves helping people
12 years grade school
4 years college
4 years medical school
3-4 years internship/residency

Optional 3-7 years fellowship
(specialty training)

Steps:

Take 1 child that loves helping people. Child goes to school. Wait 12 years. Child takes SAT. Put child in college. Wait 4 years. Child takes MCAT. Child goes to medical school. Wait 4 more years.

Final step:

Do internship, residency, and optional fellowship (3-7 years)
Child is now a DOCTOR!

These are the steps...

First is grade school. Next is high school.

Then it's college.

After that is medical school.

*Then, training school
(internship, residency, and fellowship).*

Finally, you are a DOCTOR!

Your ladder has reached into the sky.
Your journey was long and hard.

Your goal, now accomplished.
What next??

*You have more DREAMS
and build more ladders!*

*Your parents are proud
that their child is a doctor now.*

As a doctor, you'll always have a job.
You'll make a comfortable salary.

But best of all,
you'll help people feel better everyday.

So you see, you can grow up and be anything you choose to be!
A DOCTOR!

The End.